Settle In
for a quiet moment with God

Devotions *inspired* by the *wonder* of birds

Inspired by Faith

Settle in for a quiet moment with God
©Product Concept Mfg., Inc.

Settle In for a Quiet Moment with God
ISBN 978-0-9835438-6-2

Published by Product Concept Mfg., Inc.
2175 N. Academy Circle #200, Colorado Springs, CO 80909

©2011 Product Concept Mfg., Inc. All rights reserved.

All scripture quotations are from the King James version
of the Bible unless otherwise noted.

Scriptures taken from the Holy Bible,
New International Version®, NIV®.
Copyright © 1973, 1978, 1984 by Biblica, Inc.™
Used by permission of Zondervan.
All rights reserved worldwide.
www.zondervan.com

Sayings not having a credit listed are contributed by writers
for Product Concept Mfg., Inc. or in a rare case,
the author is unknown.

Written and Compiled by Patricia Mitchell
in association with Product Concept Mfg., Inc.

Settle In

for a quiet moment with God

Settle In with this book of bird inspired devotions and stories, along with thoughts from noted "birders" and others who have reflected on life and on nature, on spirituality and on the world. Discover what you can learn from birds and some of the truths they have to teach just by being themselves. Let these words bring a smile, stir a memory, inspire an idea, prompt a dream.

Settle In for a quiet moment of refreshment, entertainment, and renewal.

The Sound of Your Song

I hear your lilting song
fluttering on the breeze…
your enchanting voice draws me near,
but you are shaded
in the leafy branches
of a summer-green tree.
I listen in silence
to your sweet melodic air…
then a flash of color
darts into the sun-dipped sky…
and you disappear
while my heart applauds
in gratitude.

God has surely listened
and has heard my prayer.
-Psalm 66:19 NIV

A songbird's distinctive tune drifts through the window. We stop what we're doing and listen, transfixed by the captivating voice of the elusive creature. In a moment, she is gone, yet she leaves her song as a smile...a gift...a blessing.

As if they had wings, your prayers rise up to God. Imagine Him leaning toward the sound of your voice and listening with rapt attention to everything you want to tell Him. He's that kind of God, you know. He cares deeply about the thoughts of your heart.

Dear God, let me speak the thoughts of my heart to You with confidence, for You love to hear the sound of my voice.
Amen

The Birds Sing Here, Too

Doris Carter Wardlow

The quarter mile of jonquils he planted have bloomed and are no doubt fading, but there are more taking their place: red bud, dogwood, forsythias, crepe myrtle, and eventually the lilacs will come. These are the Mother's Day gifts he brought to me and planted a year at a time. I have now left them behind.

I haven't driven by the old farm. I don't need to. I have my 45 years of memories, both of joy and of sorrow.

How many were the mornings I would sit on the patio with my cup of coffee watching the sun come up and asking God lots of questions and asking for lots of help! I especially loved the mornings when fog rose up from the pasture and the little creek, reminding me of late years with my husband when we traveled to our beloved Scotland.

Through the mist I could hear the wild turkeys or the shrill cry of a coyote and best of all, silently witness an unsuspecting deer walking by. Always the chorus of birds lined up on the wire from the smokehouse to the house. I pampered myself into believing they performed each day just for me.

Our three children grew up there. Then there were grand-children who came later, and the farm became their dream place to visit.

Suddenly it ended. In six weeks' time near the end of my husband's life, there would be a farm equipment auction, an old farmhouse and rock outbuildings sold, and a house bought in town. There was a memorial service, and a move.

Today, I'm alone for the first time in 73 years.

One recent early morning as I sat on my sun porch—my sanctuary in this house that is now my home in town—the mist rose again and a bunny hopped across my backyard, and the birds sang. Yes, the birds sing here, too. Not the full chorus, but one by one, they performed for me.

Gradually my own heart began to sing. I knew I was not alone and would never be alone again. Where the birds sing (or even where they don't sing), God Is. And if I reach out just a wee bit, loving and caring people will be close by.

My spirit remaineth among you: fear ye not.
-Haggai 2:5

Food for Your Soul

Everybody needs
beauty as well as bread,
places to play in and pray in,
where nature may heal and
give strength to
body and soul.

-John Muir

O Lord, how manifold are thy works!
In wisdom hast thou made them all:
the earth is full of thy riches.
Psalm 104:24

The need for spiritual nourishment

is as essential as bread for the body…as seed for the sparrows…as water for the ground. Without food for the spirit, we know nothing except the physical self and the material things of this world.

To draw us toward spiritual things, God spreads before us the beauty of creation and the wonders of nature. To attract our heart and mind, He nourishes us with His presence and renews us with His promise of tender, unchangeable love.

Nourish me, dear God, with the blessing of Your presence in my life and the gift of Your wisdom in my heart.

Amen

Food for the Imagination

On one side of the window, my calico cat watches intently as sparrows, robins, woodpeckers, and jays flitter from feeder to tree, from tree to feeder. The birds pay no attention to Callie's menacing face only inches away. Somehow they know they're well protected from this well-fed, pampered predator, despite her bird-catching fantasies.

Callie isn't the only one mesmerized by the activity at the feeder. Over many summers of feeder-gazing, I'm still enchanted by my regulars...the flock of sparrows that flick more food on the ground than they eat (a bonus for the ground-feeding doves)...the scarlet cardinal and his silver-gray mate...the scrappy blue jays...the speckle-breasted woodpecker. With bird guidebook in hand, I've learned to identify birds I see less often—orioles, titmice, nuthatches, and chickadees.

The first chill of autumn tells me who my "fair-weather friends" are, and who will stick with me through winter, finding shelter in the towering pines and thick evergreens. Perhaps these sturdy souls are the ones I treasure most. When the flowers fade and the garden lies still, their fluttering and chirping around the feeder is a welcome sign of life. And while Callie may be dreaming of conquest, I am dreaming of spring.

Are we not all divine?
Are we not all made for a higher life?
-Mother Teresa

We are not human beings having a
spiritual experience. We are spiritual beings
having a human experience.
-Teilhard de Chardin

He is more within us than we are ourselves.
-Elizabeth Ann Seton

Give us this day our daily bread.
-Matthew 6:11

The beautiful vagabonds, endowed with every grace,
masters of all climes, and knowing no bounds—
how many human aspirations are realized in their free,
holiday lives—and how many suggestions
to the poet in their flight and song!
-John Burroughs

Attentive to a Happy Moment

Iridescent wings flit
across my path—
nimble beaks as delicate
as elfin slippers
nibble nectar from
trembling trumpet blossoms,
darting from one to another,
attentive to the day's business
of savoring summer's sweetness
in a flash of effervescent light.

To the attentive eye, each moment
of the year has its own beauty,
and in the same field, it beholds,
every hour, a picture which was
never seen before, and which shall
never be seen again.

-Ralph Waldo Emerson

Hummingbirds delight us as they flitter
from flower to flower, their little wings delivering them
with dizzying speed from one sweet nibble to the next.
Many times they look like a blur of frantic activity…
but if we watch carefully, we'll catch a splash of scarlet,
azure, emerald while admiring their single-minded
focus on the open-petaled blossom at hand.

Attentiveness energizes us, even when we're doing
nothing out of the ordinary. When we look for something interesting in the task at hand, we find it. When
we reach out for delight, there it is in front of us like
a wide-open flower. Attentiveness turns us from mere
doers into engaged, creative—and interesting—people.

*Dear God, open to me the beauty of this
moment, and grant me delight in the things
I do every day.*
            Amen

The Hummer's Way

The hummingbirds never seem to rest. In a flash, they catch my eye, but even before I can look up, they've dived into the lush red carpet of trumpet vine draping over my garden trellis, or shimmied into the garland's summer-kissed blossoms spilling over the flower basket.

Deterred by nothing else—not the feeder full of sunflower seeds that draw the cardinals and jays...not the grand old oak favored by nuthatches and chickadees...not the daisies dancing in the warm, fragrant breeze—the hummers impress me with their single-minded industry.

They know what they're looking for, and they go right to it!

How often I've expected sweetness to come my way, and then complain when nothing appears. I think perhaps the hummers are right: Put energy into discovering beauty. Skip whatever would drag me away from my dreams, and actively look for joy. Make happiness the day's business. That's the hummingbird's way!

It is always the simple that produces the marvelous.
-Amelia E. Barr

The Hummingbird

Emily Dickinson

A route of evanescence
With a revolving wheel;
A resonance of emerald,
A rush of cochineal;
And every blossom on the bush
Adjusts its tumbled head,–
The mail from Tunis, probably,
An easy morning's ride.

A Welcome Guest

The soul should
always stand ajar,
ready to welcome
the ecstatic experience.
-Emily Dickinson

Be not forgetful to entertain
strangers: for thereby some
have entertained angels unawares.

-Hebrews 13:2

We're a society on the move! Even if

we still live where we were born and raised, others have left to take jobs in distant cities or find adventure in faraway places. Similarly, people from other places have come into our community, enriching our lives with new perspectives, friendships, and experiences.

A spirit of hospitality keeps our eyes open for the stranger in our midst. We see her at work, church, neighborhood, or community, and we welcome her... and she's no longer a stranger, but a friend. But there's something the "stranger" can do, too. A willingness to reach out, to explore, to embrace a new place quickly turns a house into a home, a place into a community.

Let me welcome others, dear God, as You welcome me into the warm embrace of Your love.

Amen

The Woman in the Blue Dress

Carole Ann Blackley

Gerry will never forget the woman in the blue dress. Without thinking, she told the woman the seats next to her were already taken, as this table was where she and her friends always sat during Bible study. The woman appeared surprised, though she smiled graciously, picked up her purse, and rose from the chair. Gerry smiled back and didn't give it another thought until after class had begun.

Pastor opened the class by asking if there were any visitors present, and Gerry noticed a blue-clad arm peek out from one of the back tables. At that moment, comments she had heard about her church being unfriendly came to mind. Cold. Cliquish. Unwelcoming. All those words flew at her like a flock of squawking crows to their roost. Suddenly it wasn't "the church" or "the congregation"—it was she.

When class ended, Gerry got up immediately, waved goodbye to her friends, and wove through the crowd in search of the woman in the blue dress. She had left the room. Gerry rushed out to the parking lot, but the woman was nowhere to be seen. Every Sunday for months after, Gerry scanned the congregation for her, hoping against hope to see her, but she never did.

"I've always thought of myself as a generous person," Gerry told me later. "My friends can depend on me, and I volunteer my time to the church. I scatter seed for the birds, I put out food for the animals—I'm not selfish!" But an uncomfortable fact remained: When it came down to giving a simple thing like a place at the table for a woman sitting all by herself, she had failed completely.

That's how Gerry became the woman not only her friends could depend on, but visitors, too. She goes out of her way to greet them, ask their name and where they're from. Sure, not a few times she has welcomed a longtime member of her large congregation, but she has learned to laugh. And of course, she would rather spend all her time chatting with her friends, but she has learned to give the gift every newcomer longs for—a touch of genuine hospitality.

Hospitality invites to prayer before it checks credentials, welcomes to the table before administering the entrance exam.

-Patrick Henry

Kindness is the language which the deaf can hear
and the blind can see.
-Mark Twain

Good judgment comes from experience,
and experience comes from poor judgment.
-Saying

Let truth and love and honor and courtesy
flow in all thy deeds.
-Ralph Waldo Emerson

Much misconstruction and bitterness
are spared to him who thinks naturally upon
what he owes to others, rather than on what he
ought to expect from them.
-Elizabeth de Meulan Guizot

Be kindly affectioned one to another with brotherly
love; in honour preferring one another.
-Romans 12:10

A mysterious bond of brotherhood makes all men one.
-Thomas Carlyle

Our deeds still travel with us from afar, and what we
have been makes us what we are.
-George Eliot

I was thirsty, and ye gave me drink:
I was a stranger, and ye took me in.
-Matthew 25:35

Sow good service;
sweet remembrances will grow from them.
-Madame de Staël

People may forget what you said,
and they may forget what you did but they will never
ever forget the way you made them feel.
-Saying

The Comfort of a Sheltered Place

How do you fare,
little robin,
when thunder scatters
the flock and wild winds
bend the tall willow tree?
You have all disappeared,
chased by scowling clouds
sheeting the garden with rain.
Then, clouds part...
quietude returns.
A brave ray of sunshine
bathes the stillness
in fresh translucent light...
and you skip out to pluck your
meal from soft, luxuriant soil.

In the Lord put I my trust.
-Psalm 11:1

When the rain falls, it brings the
pleasure of a watered garden to one...the problem
of a leaking roof to another. When the sun shines,
it provides a glorious day outdoors for one...
a gnawing thirst for another.

When life's "weather" seems to bring you more
hardships than benefits...more anxiety than joy...
God opens His arms to you as your shelter and
refuge. He tenderly invites you to receive His
soothing care, and to rest in His peace, even
though storms rage around you.

From your new vantage point, you may see what
you have never noticed before—a patch of blue
sky...a ray of sunshine...goodness to hold in
both hands.

Shelter me, dear God, when life's storms
threaten me, and grant me peace.
Amen

The Gentle Giant

Polly M. Richmond

I loved my grandma more than I can say, but when I was little, her big, rambling house scared me to death. From its dark, cob-webby basement to its shadowy, musty attic, rooms teemed with murmured secrets and long-lost family lore. Nooks and closets, I was sure, housed ghosts that roamed the halls as soon as darkness fell.

Whenever my big sister and I stayed overnight, Grandma would offer us two upstairs bedrooms, each with a four-poster bed piled with plump pillows and draped with flowery patchwork quilts…a sit-down vanity, and dainty ladies writing desk. But we begged to share a room, never revealing the true reason to Grandma, or to each other: in the dark hours of night, we sought safety in numbers against the ghosts and goblins…but especially against the giant oak tree.

Right outside our room it stood. Like mighty arms upraised in battle, its branches loomed into the sky, and its leaves hid any number of menacing things. In the moonlight, it cast shivering shadows on the walls of our room as we huddled together. In summer storms, its branches groaned like banshees on the prowl.

The year I turned ten, my sister went to camp for a week, and I stayed at Grandma's house. Determined to show how grown-up I was, I confidently followed Grandma upstairs to the familiar bedroom and put my backpack on the desk. "You tidy up," Grandma said, "and I'll go back down to the kitchen and get our lunch ready."

As the stairs creaked with her disappearing footsteps, I looked at the familiar room. "There are no ghosts in here!" I told myself, hoping my words alerted any loitering ghosts. I stood by the open window, and defiantly stared at the big old oak. Then I spied it—a tiny bird's nest cupped in a nook of branches, sheltered by a roof of lush springtime leaves. A mother bird sat, her eyes darting to me in a frightened stare.

"I won't hurt you, Mama Bird," I whispered, as I tip-toed from the spot and made my way to the kitchen.

That night, I crawled into the four-poster bed, resolved to brave the darkness alone. I closed my eyes and fell asleep until—Boom! Crack! Flash! I shot upright. Lightning flashed, punctuated by peal after peal of thunder. I heard the wind whip through the oak tree and long branches slap across the window. "Mama Bird!" I cried aloud. I imagined her terror, her nest tumbling down, her eggs crushed, her family gone.

At last, the storm passed and I fell into a fitful sleep. When I awoke, the window was glistening with sun-kissed raindrops, and the oak sparkled with freshly washed purity. At once I sprang out of bed and dashed to the window, looking down first to confirm my fears—but no nest lay on the ground. Then I looked up and peered into the branches. There she was, her nest intact, Mama's eggs snuggly beneath her sheltering breast! Papa Bird flitted to her side with a morsel in his mouth. I smiled ear-to-ear.

The ancient oak looked more like a gentle giant than a menacing ogre...a protective embrace than a tentacled monster. And every night that week, whenever I would feel afraid, I simply looked out the window to the oak that shielded Mama Bird...and would surely shelter me.

God is our refuge and strength,
a very present help in trouble.
-Psalm 46:1

His eye is on the SPARROW

1905 Hymn
Lyrics: Civilla Martin
Comp: Charles Gabriel

Why should I feel discouraged,
why should the shadows come,
Why should my heart be lonely,
and long for heaven and home,
When Jesus is my portion?
My constant friend is He:
His eye is on the sparrow,
and I know He watches me;
His eye is on the sparrow,
and I know He watches me.

Refrain:
I sing because I'm happy,
I sing because I'm free,
For His eye is on the sparrow,
And I know He watches me.

The Blessing of a Kindly Word

That's the wise thrush;
he sings each song twice over,
Lest you should think he
never could recapture
The first fine careless rapture!

-Robert Browning

A word aptly spoken is like apples
of gold in settings of silver.

-Proverbs 25:11 NIV

When birds of all kinds cluster around the feeder, our eyes are drawn first to the ones we find most interesting—the delicate goldfinch, the spotted woodpecker, the scarlet cardinal. But the scene would lose its richness without a crowd of common sparrows, whose feisty ways and familiar call are part of nature's abundance.

In a similar way, our ears are drawn first to words that pique our interest…ease our way…encourage our efforts…inspire our heart…enlighten our mind. They're memorable words, often from the lips of prominent or influential people.

Yet it's often plain, simple, heartfelt "sparrow" words that mean the most, coming to us from people who care about us. Words from people we see every day… people just like you.

Dear God, grant me the opportunity to bless someone with my words today.
Amen

Spring Is Here

Madison McRobert

We were newlyweds when my husband lost his job. Only months earlier, we had moved into our dream home in rural Louisiana. The tall windows of my art studio looked out onto a small garden where we set up a variety of bird feeders to hold finch food, hummingbird nectar, sunflower seeds, and a songbird mix. I had started my first canvas inspired by the bucolic scene right in front of my eyes when he came home with the news.

After several months of fear and uncertainty, he was hired by a company in Chicago. Of course we were thrilled he had found work so soon, but packing up for the move was the hardest thing I've ever had to do. I could hardly glance at the garden without crying. I couldn't bring myself to take down the feeders. On the morning we were to leave, I filled them as full as I could get them, whispering a painful farewell to my gathering diners as they flitted, oblivious to my tears, through the bushes and trees.

Chicago-area home prices stunned us, but we managed to find a small house with enough space for my studio, along with a small fenced-in yard. Summer flowers, planted by the

previous owner, brightened the patio, and several hooks
and posts for feeders had been placed around the tiny lawn.
My husband and I bought new feeders, along with seed to
attract the birds of the region.

In late August, flocks of blackbirds started descending
on our feeders, emptying the seed within the space of an
afternoon. Then they'd lift into the air in a chorus of caws
and cries—I realized they were saying, "So long! So long!"
And one morning, they were gone, followed by our other
feathered friends in the weeks to come. The garden turned
still and quiet.

Snows fell particularly heavily that year, and by March, I
was wishing I could have followed the blackbirds to whatever sunny destination they had chosen. The stark white
landscape with its eerie silence closed in on me, and though
I knew with my head that spring was almost here, my heart
could not believe it—until—

Another cold morning, the low sun barely lightening the
leaden sky. "Cheer up! cheer up!" I rushed to the window,
and there she was, a little robin skittering across the ground
to a small patch of lawn where snow had melted! Her words
floated like music through the air—words even my heart
understood. It was high time to fill the feeders again!

A World of Simple Wonders

I have found a quiet place...
the trill of cellphones
an unwelcome intruder,
the hum of the highway
a distant whisper.
Yes, I have found this place
where the trees shade
and a pond glistens
in lifting mist
and a heron stands silently
at water's edge
surveying the landscape
of another tranquil day.

Bird watching is an activity open to almost everyone. From tiny, window-mounted feeders to elaborate garden birdhouses...from views through a pane of glass to sightings in a nature sanctuary...bird watching provides hours of delight, entertainment, and discovery.

Though we have many options available, simple pleasures so often are the best. They don't depend on fancy equipment, come with a thick instruction booklet, need batteries, or ask for our charge card.

Simple pleasures are the ones God created, and He has given them to each of us for free.

Thank You, dear God, for the beauty and wonder of Your creation.

Amen

A Time to See

T. R. Cunningham

The only thing I knew about the woman who lived next door was that she had a lot of bird feeders. Feeders of all types and sizes hung in rows from her deck and perched on various posts placed around her yard. Occasionally I'd see her out filling the feeders and we'd wave, but that's about it. I was in my twenties, just starting my career; I left early in the morning, and I rarely got home from work before 7 or 8 o'clock at night.

One Monday morning, very early, I woke to the wail of sirens and the glare of flashing lights swirling around the walls of my room. I threw on some clothes and rushed outside just as medics were maneuvering a gurney down the stairs of my neighbor's house and into an ambulance. I learned from another neighbor that she—Mrs. Williamson—had fallen, but had managed to call 911. She was being taken to a local hospital for X-rays. I expressed sympathy, then went back inside and got ready for the work day.

When I pulled in the driveway that evening, Mrs. Williamson stepped out onto her porch, one arm encased in a sling. She motioned for me to come over. After talking briefly about what had happened, she paused, and then said, "I won't be able to lift both my arms for at least a month… and I was wondering…I was wondering…that is, if you have time…if you would come over in the mornings and fill my bird feeders."

"Sure," I replied, though with more excitement than I actually felt. But I had said yes, and she told me where she kept the tin of seed.

Before work the next morning, I stepped over to Mrs. Williamson's patio, found the tin, opened it, and filled a big scoop with seed. One by one, I topped each feeder, making several trips back to the tin before I was finished. Then I hurried off to work.

By the third or fourth day, I realized that birds were chattering up in the trees as I went about my task. Another day, and they swooped down, clambering over the feeders before I had even stepped out of the yard.

On Saturday, I stopped to watch them for a few minutes—then I lingered a few more minutes, mesmerized by their energy, vibrancy, and variety. I sat down on a lawn chair and continued to watch, amazed that so many different kinds of birds lived right around me. I had had no idea!

Almost without a sound, the patio door slid open and Mrs. Williamson slipped out. She smiled, sat down, and we both watched birds. That was the beginning of a warm friendship, as well as a hobby that continues to bring me relaxation and pleasure to this day.

I once had a sparrow alight upon my shoulder for a
moment, while I was hoeing in a village garden,
and I felt that I was more distinguished by that
circumstance than I should have been by any epaulet
I could have worn.
                    -Henry David Thoreau

I hope you love birds too. It is economical.
It saves going to heaven.
-Emily Dickinson

Purity and simplicity are the two wings with which
man soars above the earth.
-Thomas à Kempis

Why not learn to enjoy the little things?
There are so many of them!
-Author unknown

In character, in manners, in style; in all things,
the supreme excellence is simplicity.
-Henry Wadsworth Longfellow

I never for a day gave up listening to the songs of our
birds, or watching their peculiar habits, or delineating
them in the best way I could.
-John James Audubon

Blessed are the simple in heart,
for they shall have much peace.
-Thomas à Kempis

In Gratitude for Today's Blessings

The fountain of
contentment must
spring up in the mind;
and he who has so little
knowledge of human
nature as to seek
happiness by changing
anything but his own
disposition, will waste
his life in fruitless efforts
and multiply the griefs
which he proposes
to remove.

-Samuel Johnson

Godliness with contentment
is great gain.

-1 Timothy 6:6

"A bird in the hand is worth two in the bush," as the saying goes. Certainly what we can see, touch, hear, and feel now merits our attention, more than what would have been, if...more than what could be tomorrow, provided.... Yet so often these are the things we think about.

Contentment means letting go of the past and allowing the future to unfold. It means knowing what we can control...and what we cannot. Most of all, it means acknowledging the wrongs, fixing what we're able to fix...and rejoicing in the good, giving thanks for all that makes each life a unique gift from our loving God.

Open my eyes to see and my arms to embrace the blessings from Your hand today, dear God.
                        Amen

The Condo

Polly M. Richmond

"We could put up a purple martin house!" I exclaimed enthusiastically to my less-than-enthused husband. From long experience, he knew that "we" meant "you," and he had already dug holes and poured cement bases for a finch feeder, two sunflower seed feeders, three bluebird houses, and one large mixed seed feeder. But my sweetheart dutifully followed me to the tree-free spot in our yard where I thought the martin house should go, and he set up a pole.

Early that spring, I hoisted the two-story condo-style house up to its towering location, and attached a baffle near the bottom of the pole to deter raccoons. Then I waited for the arrival of my first family of martins.

Purple martins are noted for their airborne acrobatics, swooping high and low in elegant arcs and graceful loops and twirls. Once a pair establishes a nesting place, they return year after year to raise their young.

What I didn't know then was this: it's not easy to attract a pair. Martins, belonging to the swallow family, are easily elbowed out of potential nesting places by starlings. Would-be martin landlords need to remove nests started by these more aggressive birds, daily if necessary, until they get the message and move on.

But I stood by and watched as several starlings busily carried leaves and twigs up to the condo, each bird claiming her space in one of a dozen rooms available. After a week or so, I could see bits of grass sticking out of inhabited spaces, and occasionally glimpse a mama's face peeking out from her nest. One evening, perched on the condo's porch, a big starling stood, looking proprietarily over the length and breadth of his estate.

"We've got a starling house," I announced to my husband, but what I really meant was "I've got a starling house." I had jumped into the project before finding out what I needed to know, and now I couldn't bring myself to destroy the starlings' nests. I watched the males deliver food to their mates, and then heard the chirps of newborn chicks. Later the chicks ventured out onto the condo porch...with a little nudging from Mom, they took to the air and discovered they could fly.

Yes, I know—those irascible, bully-bird starlings are no one's favorites—but when the condo fell silent and flocks of starlings started swooping into the sky at the first touch of chill to the air, I waved farewell. "You weren't purple martins," I said, "but you were mine for a season."

It is no use to grumble and complain;
It's just as cheap and easy to rejoice;
When God sorts out the weather and sends rain—
Why, rain's my choice.
               -James Whitcomb Riley

I value my garden more for being full of blackbirds
than of cherries, and very frankly give them fruit for
their songs.

-Joseph Addison

*Happy the man who early learns the wide chasm that
lies between his wishes and his powers.*

-Johann Wolfgang von Goethe

We are made for God and will be dissatisfied until we
have God in our hearts.

-Augustine

*I make the most of all that comes
and the least of all that goes.*

-Sara Teasdale

It's not what happens to you,
but how you react to it that matters.

-Epictetus

*Adapt yourself to the things among which your lot has
been cast and love sincerely the fellow creatures with
whom destiny has ordained that you shall live.*

-Marcus Aurelius

A Sweet Awaking to a New Day

Rays of pale dawn,
like a bashful child,
extend a wistful gaze
across the garden.
Still innocent,
still charged with
untold possibilities,
the hour unfolds
to the cry of a crow
in the far-off distance
and a chorus of sparrows replies
from the boughs
of dew-charmed trees.

It could be as simple as an early-morning stroll or an after-dinner walk around the neighborhood. Or an afternoon break enjoying a cup of coffee...or a leisurely hot bath before going to bed. We need a little "time out" each day to de-stress and replenish our strength and energy.

A few quiet moments just to be with yourself renews body and soul, mind and spirit. A little bit of time out has the power to center your thoughts and enlarge your perspective...to revitalize you for the task that lies ahead...to relax you for a night of peaceful sleep.

Dear God, help me make time to care for my
physical and spiritual needs.
Amen

Air Power

Howard "Chip" Shaw III

One bright summer morning my little dog Rosa and I went out for a stroll. We had been experiencing a drought for some time, but several days earlier, monsoon-like storms arrived and this day was cool and wet under a clear blue sky. Every living thing seemed to be charged with renewed energy from the recent downpours of life-giving rain.

I decided to walk up to a high point on the red rocks where we could see if the rain had filled a small basin that was once a pond. As we approached the spot with a view of the valley, something like a whirlwind engulfed us. The atmosphere was transformed and darkened as fast-moving, daredevil swallows surrounded us. These black, gray and white precision-flyers darted and zoomed past us as if we were statues.

My dog and I both stood stock still as a spectacular air show developed. Hundreds of birds performed a beautifully cho-reographed routine in front of us, beside us, above, below

48

and behind us. I watched in complete awe as I noticed a small flying insect, back lit by the sun, move slowly upward. As it got close to my eye level, a bird that was flying toward me banked quickly, captured the insect in its beak, and then vanished from sight.

I shifted my attention to the sounds. The extreme quiet of the morning was replaced with the indescribable sounds of these amazing aviators in flight. Like miniature jet planes they whooshed, zoomed, and whistled as they pierced the air around us. I must have been standing there perfectly still for at least five minutes, watching and listening, when I realized that I was as calm and relaxed as I ever remember being.

This experience was clearly a gift from God, and I will never forget what I saw and how I felt that day. I know that He takes care of multitudes of little birds and that he is also watching over me, providing all of the things I need to work through life's greatest challenges.

New Ways for a New Day

Birds knew the meaning
of "repurpose" long
before the word appeared
in articles about frugality
and thrift.
A trellis holds
a robin's nest...
an old shed
harbors wrens...
and long utility wires
make a very fine perch
for sparrows on the wing.

When the landscape changes, it's easy to lose our bearings. Events transform our familiar world into a frightening, confusing place. As attitudes and expectations shift through the years, we often don't know what to make of it all.

A willingness to adapt to circumstances is not always easy, yet adaptability allows us to move forward with confidence and grace. New ways of doing things? We can learn them and find how they benefit us. New tools and technology? We can use them to enrich our lives.

Nonetheless, one thing remains the same—God and His love for you. That's something you can depend on today, tomorrow, and forever.

Thank You, dear God, for the assurance
of Your continuing, unchangeable love.
Amen

View from the Wire

Roberta Kimball-Smith

I had come back to visit an elderly neighbor, and the elms were gone. Block after block of nothing but bare lawns, and a few saplings struggling to make it through the dry summer. Elm disease had decimated the trees that used to line each side of the road. Dappled light through a fresh green canopy of spring was now a memory of the past, along with carefree bike rides to the dime store and long summer afternoons playing hide-and-seek with the other kids on the block.

As I opened my former neighbor's garden gate, I looked up. There I saw dozens of birds lined up like a row of pegs along the utility wires. Yes, their lofty perches had disappeared when the trees came down. I couldn't help but admire their easy adaptability.

Little did I know then how much adaptability I would need in years to come! Like many baby boomers, I stepped from an innocent, peaceful time into an era of increasing unrest… from a world where roles and expectations were set to a world offering broad possibilities. From a boxy, black rotary phone wired to the wall to a phone the size of a deck of cards I slip in my purse…from pecking at the keyboard of my mom's manual typewriter to sending electronic documents from my PC.

Of course, we were by no means the first generation to greet new inventions, nor the first to experience social change. Think what it must have been like for men and women during the Industrial Revolution—they expected to produce goods by hand, either at home or on the farm. Instead, they found themselves in factories working long hours in the din of hot, dangerous machinery. Or for families and nations throughout the ages and to this day displaced by war, famine, and other calamities.

Perhaps, however, we're the first generation called to adapt so many times to so many things throughout the years of our lives. We've seen things we used to take for granted gone in the space of a few years. We've returned to school to learn skills we couldn't possibly have known we'd need—and some of us more than once! And who hasn't asked a son or daughter or grandchild how to download files or find information on the Internet?

How have you navigated change? Chances are, you simply do what the birds do: if you find that the familiar trees are gone, you find a wire to perch on while you look over your new landscape. And likely, too, you've been surprised and delighted by what you've seen!

Everything is changing; God alone is changeless.
-Teresa of Avila

Plan Your Work...
Work Your Plan

No bird soars too
high if he soars with
his own wings.

-William Blake

Let us run with perseverance
the race marked out for us.

-Hebrews 12:1 NIV

After the thrill of naming a goal

and planning how to achieve it, comes the day-to-day business of bringing it to reality. Drudgery? Certainly not! Each day, every hour that we spend doing what it takes to get us there is a day, an hour, well spent.

Where would you like to be a year from now? How could you make this happen? And most importantly— what are you going to do every day that will put you closer to your goal? Even if your steps are small (and often small steps are the steadiest steps), persever- ance turns today's dreams into tomorrow's actuality.

Dear God, grant me the resolve it takes to make my plans succeed, according to Your good will.

Amen

Not a Sparrow Falls

Doris Carter Wardlow

One day, when the kids were little and we were all living in the old farmhouse, I discovered that the telephone was out of order. From a neighbor's house, I called the phone company, and soon a repairman arrived. It didn't take him long to find the problem.

A little bird mother had built her nest in the box that held phone wires going into the house. When the repairman peered into the nest, five little open beaks reached up for the repairman to feed them. Three tender-hearted children watched, concerned.

"If I move them," the repairman said, "the mother bird won't claim them."

"Why not set the nest down in the bushes? Maybe she'll find them," suggested one of the children.

"Oh, but the kitty cats would have a feast if we do that," the repairman replied. He was right. There were many kitty cats around.

"Well, I think the only chance they have is if we put the nest as high as possible in the elm tree, and hope for the best," I said. And that's what we did.

The repairman gently lifted the nest of chirping chicks out of the phone box and handed it to the youngest boy. Meanwhile, the oldest boy climbed partway up the elm, and the nest with its five tiny babes was carefully handed to him. He climbed as high as he could to find the safest bough for the nest. He hoped the worried mother bird was watching.

The two younger children sat on the back porch, praying their own open-hearted little prayers that this mother would not reject the nest, now touched by human hands, but would "break the rules" of nature and return to her babies.

The oldest boy hurried back down the tree, took his place with the little congregation on the porch, and watched. Lo and behold – in no time, the mother bird flew back to the nest with food in her beak. The family was happily together again.

> *Give thanks to the God of heaven.*
> *His love endures forever.*
> *-Psalm 136:26 NIV*

A Delightful Frolic

Water-fluttered feathers
scatter rainbows
into the sky
as a lone jay splashes
with the glee
of a toddler homed in on
a rippling puddle.
Water everywhere!
And the thrill of delight
lingers long into
the summer afternoon.

Every good gift and every
perfect gift is from above…

-James 1:17

It's not hard to think of something that delights–the face of a loved one…a phone call from a friend…a thrilling surprise…a blossom on a spring day. Whatever might have been causing us concern only a moment before suddenly vanishes, and we feel happy, heartwarming delight from head to toe.

Did you know that "delight" describes the way God feels toward you? He loves His creation, and He has created you. He knows you better than anyone else possibly could, and He blesses you daily. Why? Simply because He delights in you.

Thank You, dear God, for looking on me with delight!

Amen

To Everything... A Purpose

Patricia Mitchell

Though the robin frolicked with unfettered frenzy in the cool, fresh water, a sense of calmness slipped over me as I watched her play. Her seeming pleasure in the few inches of water I had put out that morning gratified me, and I couldn't help but set aside what I was doing, sit down, and savor the moment.

The robin's enjoyment reminded me of the time a friend noticed a piece of needlework I had in my hand. "What do you plan to do with that?" she queried as she peered at my tiny, slow-going stitches. Truly, the project had no particular purpose beyond allowing me to practice an appliqué technique I had learned at a recent workshop. Whenever I finished, perhaps I could make it into a pillow or a wall hanging or a label for a larger piece or...

My friend's implied meaning—why in the world are you doing this?—got me thinking. Why, indeed? Why did two dozen women spend an entire afternoon with a noted quilting teacher to learn her method and practice her technique? Why do I spend evenings hand-stitching a design when machines can whip out decorative panels in minutes?

Perhaps for the same reason the robin splashes in the bird bath until only a few drops of water remain. I like creating with threads and fabric, and if something pleasing emerges, so much the better. And who knows? I just might find a purpose for it someday!

To every thing there is a season,
and a time to every purpose under the heaven.
-Ecclesiastes 3:1

You cannot prevent the birds of sorrow from flying
over your head, but you can prevent them
from building a nest there.
-Proverb

There is no duty we so underrate
as the duty of being happy.
-Robert Louis Stevenson

The Lord thy God in the midst of thee is mighty;
he will save, he will rejoice over thee with joy; he will
rest in his love, he will joy over thee with singing.
-Zephaniah 3:17

A bird does not sing because it has an answer.
It sings because it has a song.
-Proverb

Unique in so Many Ways

I care not so much
what I am to others
as what I am to myself.
I will be rich by myself,
and not by borrowing.

-Montaigne

To love others, we must first
learn to love ourselves.

-Proverb

Have you ever wished to be someone else?
At one time or another, most of us have. Compared
to a person we find glamorous, talented, influential,
or privileged, we're apt to rate ourselves pretty low!
That's why we need to hear it again and again: each
one of us has unique strengths...particular gifts...and a
singular, God-given place and purpose in the world.

Sure, it's thrilling to meet charismatic people who
motivate you to do your best, and it's inspiring to meet
someone who encourages you to grow. But then, come
home...come home to the exquisite person you are,
and be glad for the corner of the world that only you
can fill.

*Dear God, You have made me to be Yours...
and I am blessed.*

Amen

Birds of the Bible

What kind of bird are you—bashful sparrow or rowdy jay? Soaring falcon or land-loving robin? Happy-go-lucky songbird or sagacious owl?

Through traits traditionally attributed to various birds, the Bible teaches us about God—and about ourselves. Here are a few examples:

An eagle portrays God's power and strength. God is able to lift us up even more easily than an eagle can pluck a twig from a tree and carry it to her nest. As her great wings protect her young from harm, so God's love and compassion shelter us from danger and despair.

He shall cover thee with his feathers, and under his wings shalt thou trust: his truth shall be thy shield and buckler.
Psalm 91:4

The Bible helps us comprehend the gentleness of His Spirit when He is likened to a dove descending on Jesus at the time of His baptism:

When He had been baptized, Jesus came up immediately from the water; and behold, the heavens were opened to Him, and He saw the Spirit of God descending like a dove and alighting upon Him.
Matthew 3:16

Later in His ministry, Jesus pointed to the dove, a symbol of peace, to remind us that we are to be people of peace, innocent of initiating quarrels and giving offense to others:

> *Be ye therefore wise as serpents,*
> *and harmless as doves.*
> *Matthew 10:16*

He also cited the sparrow—"a dime a dozen!" we might say today—to illustrate how much each one of us means to Him and how much He cares.

> *Are not two sparrows sold for a penny?*
> *Yet not one of them will fall to the ground outside*
> *of your Father's care. And even the very hairs*
> *of your head are all numbered. So don't be afraid;*
> *you are worth more than many sparrows.*
> *Matthew 10:29-31 NIV*

And there's something else we can pick up from the Bible's bird talk: Each bird is different. Each possesses distinct features, characteristics, attributes, and beauty. Each lends its own strengths and its own distinctiveness to the world... and in the same way, that's how it is with us. We each count...we each contribute...we each matter to God, and to each other.

> *Let us remember that within us*
> *there is a palace of immense magnificence.*
> *Teresa of Avila*

Abundant Blessings in a World of Plenty

The daily ritual begins.
A sparrow is the first
to land in the place
where seed is spread,
and deftly pecks his
favored morsel.
Then a robin sails in,
and sparrow darts
away; a jay arrives
soon displaced by
starlings on the watch
for food.
"There's plenty,"
I want to cry, but
I know the birds
will have it only
their chosen way.

"Count your blessings!" So often we count them only when things are going wrong. We want to balance the bad with the good, the losses with the gains. Enumerating what's going right can give us the perspective we need to successfully face our challenges.

But why not count them when things are going right... when God sends a special gift into our lives? We are filled with joy, and our "counting" becomes a prayer of thanksgiving. "Not only this blessing," we might proclaim, "but that blessing, and that blessing, too!"

Even more is an ordinary day a time to think of His blessings—the sky and earth, the flowers and trees, the birds and animals we love. All these are blessings—all these are reasons to give Him thanks.

Dear God, thank You for all you have made,
and for all you have given to me in my life.
Amen

Plenty for All

Madison McRobert

It's not always a pretty picture when wild birds squabble
for space at the feeder. Chirps turn to squawks, big birds
swoop down as little birds scatter, and the bellicose among
them perch where they please, the space occupied or not.
Compelled by nature, wild birds compete for scarce food by
getting all they can, when they can.

Competitiveness is part of our nature, too. As very young
children, we develop our sense of self and a clear conviction
of what's "mine"—which is usually anything that catches our
eye, regardless of prior ownership. Later, we learn to "play
nice," respecting the difference between our possessions
and those of other people. What we don't always leave
behind, however, is a sense of scarcity—the idea that there's
only so much to go around, and if we want something we
must get it away from someone else, or beat others to the
prize.

A sense of scarcity leads us to regard others as competitors
for "a place on the perch." We imagine we have to fight for
our share of the good life, all the while ignoring a central
truth: Before we were born, God made a place for each of
us. He provided us with all we need to live at peace with
Him and with others...to fulfill His purpose...to live the true
good life in Him.

Yes, we want to open our arms and embrace all the physical blessings God puts in front of us every day. But there's no reason at all to elbow someone else out of the way, nor is there reason to shrink back if someone else happens to come along beside us.

God never scrimps on blessings. There's plenty—more than plenty!—for you...for all.

Thou preparest a table before me in the presence of mine enemies: thou anointest my heard with oil;
my cup runneth over.
-Psalm 23:5

Now there are diversities of gifts, but the same Spirit.
-1 Corinthians 12:4

Happier of happy though I be, like them I cannot take possession of the sky, mount with a thoughtless impulse, and wheel there, one of a mighty multitude whose way and motion is a harmony and dance magnificent.
-William Wordsworth

Many Happy Returns

With the first budding tree...,
the barest hint of green
through winter's frost,
they come.
Morning by morning,
the song builds
and soon its melody
has lured them back,
all those who have spent
the bleak months
in greener hills.

It's easy to imagine God, bigger than nature itself, welcoming all who come to Him as sunshine beckons birds to come and stay. It's easy to picture ourselves flying directly into His wide-open arms and basking in the warmth of His peace!

But now let's turn the picture around. Imagine yourself—your heart—as a place in nature. Imagine God as a tiny sparrow taking it upon Himself to come to you. What season will He find? Will He be turned away by the chill of unbelief, or welcomed by the sweet breath of spring?

In nature, a sparrow has no power to change winter to spring; but God does. He comes humbly, ready to touch your heart with new, green, blossoming life in Him.

> *Let the season of my heart, dear God,
> welcome Your presence.*
> *Amen*

Back to the Beginning

Roberta Cresswell

The report was due tomorrow, and I needed hours of uninterrupted time to crunch numbers, calculate percentages, and prepare graphs and pie charts. That's why I called the agency and told my boss I would be working at home today. Then I sat down at the kitchen table with a mug of coffee, opened my laptop, and got straight to work.

My mind swimming in numbers, I barely noticed the morning shadows giving way to sunshine pouring across the patio. I was barely conscious of all the chirping, peeping, and fluttering on the other side of a single sliding glass door.

By noon, my shoulders ached and my head throbbed. "Good grief!" I said to myself, "I need to relax! I need a vacation, and soon!" Yet I knew this was only a pipedream, because the next several months were the agency's busy season, and no one (at least anyone who valued his or her job) ever took time off right now.

"Okay, 20 minutes, tops!" I vowed as I pulled sandwich fixings from the fridge and grabbed a soda. After stacking cheese, deli meat, and lettuce between two slices of bread, I took my lunch back to the table and sat down, resisting the urge to scan spreadsheets while I chewed.

Instead, I looked out to the patio. And there they were—a bunch of birds, from jays to chickadees, all crowding around the feeder. I watched, almost mesmerized by the cacophony of sounds and the carefree frolic taking place outside.

Three-quarters of an hour passed before I thought to look at the time. My headache gone and shoulders relaxed, I felt refreshed, as if, well, I had just taken a vacation. Minus, of course, the expense and a week away from work!

I got the message. I like my job, and a fast-paced workplace energizes me. But somewhere along the line, I lost what I knew as a child—I need space to simply watch and listen to what's around me. That's where refreshment comes from, and refreshment is important, no matter when the reports are due. (And I finished this one with time to spare!)

For, lo, the winter is past, the rain is over and gone;
The flowers appear on the earth;
the time of the singing of birds is come,
and the voice of the turtle is heard in our land.
-Song of Solomon 2:11-12

Work, alternated with needful rest,
is the salvation of man or woman.
-Antoinette Brown Blackwell

Stepping Outside Your Comfort Zone

The fishermen know
that the sea is dangerous
and the storm terrible,
but they have never found
these dangers sufficient reason
for remaining ashore.

-Vincent van Gogh

Be strong in the Lord,
and in the power of his might.

-Ephesians 6:10

"Take a chance!" or "Stay safe!" If you're like
most people, you've heard both kinds of advice. You've
been urged to "step outside your comfort zone," but
not to "do something foolish"...to "go for it," but "know
your limits."

God would have you embrace all those things, yet hold
them with the mind of His wisdom and in the perspective of His truth. He offers you both the confidence to
step into new opportunities and the conviction to step
away from wrongdoing...the courage to take calculated
risks and the prudence to avoid perilous situations.

With God as your guide, you can thrill to the excitement of stepping out, of doing something different, of
taking a risk, of following your dreams, of doing what
you believe possible...because you know, no matter
what happens, He will be there for you.

I pray, dear God, for Your guidance
as I follow my goals and dreams.
Amen

Going Places

Roberta Kimball-Smith

"What's the worst that can happen?" I ask myself that question whenever I'm facing a new situation. It all goes back to the time I joined a friend of mine and her family on a bird-sighting outing.

My friend, Fran, and I were both ten years old, but at opposite ends of the spectrum—or the bird—when it came to knowing about birds. Fran stood at the head, able to name everything from finches to cranes with barely a thought. I, however, stood at the tail. I hadn't paid attention to birds beyond our neighbor's pair of parakeets.

Yet I went on the walk anyway, cocksure I could mask my ignorance, maybe even picking up a few bird names I could rattle off as if I had known them all along. How quickly my adolescent arrogance turned to mortification!

As soon as we entered the park, Fran's parents suggested we pair off and see how many birds each team of two could spot. Fran's mom got out two notebooks and gave one to us, and then we were on our own. "Poor Fran!" I thought. "She's going to lose this game...and hate me for being so stupid."

We started out on a trail. The Christmassy smell of pine trees enveloped us, and the peeps of birdsong made us stop and listen. "That sounds like a redwing blackbird to me," Fran said in a whisper. "Uh-huh," I replied.

"Look! There it is!" she whispered again, pointing toward what to me looked like a streak from one tree to the next. Fran gleefully scribbled "redwing blackbird" in her notebook. From there we—or I should say, she—spotted blue jays, kestrels, woodpeckers, and hawks. A deer scampered across our path, followed by her long-legged fawn. Soon enchanted, I forgot about myself and tried as hard as I could to spot the elusive flyers. Fran, so caught up in the thrill, didn't even seem to notice that I contributed nothing to the notebook, but kept asking, "What's that? What's that sound like?"

After an hour, we met up with her parents and found that our lists were nearly identical. A tie, it was decided. But on the way home, I had to fess up. "This is the first time I've done this," I said, "and Fran knew all the birds."

"Oh, that's okay," her mom laughed. "What's important is this—did you have a good time?"

"Oh yes!" I exclaimed truthfully. "I learned about birds, saw them, and heard them. Fran is really smart!" My friend blushed, but I could tell she was pleased.

Before I was dropped off at my house, Fran's mom drew out a book from her tote bag. "Here's a guide to birds in our area," she said. "You can borrow it, and the next time we take a bird walk, you will know as much as Fran—maybe even more!"

Yes, I learned about birds that day, and also to appreciate what others could teach me. I learned that doing something different—going someplace I've never been before—can be the start of something wonderful!

> *To avoid an occasion for our virtues is a worse degree of failure than to push forward pluckily and make a fall.*
> *-Robert Louis Stevenson*

Finite to fail, but infinite to venture.
-Emily Dickinson

Prudence keeps life safe,
but does not often make it happy.
-Samuel Johnson

Do the hardest thing on earth for you.
Act for yourself. Face the truth.
-Katherine Mansfield

Mix a little foolishness with your prudence:
It's good to be silly at the right moment.
-Horace

Finish each day and be done with it.
You have done what you could. Some blunders and
absurdities no doubt crept in; forget them
as soon as you can. Tomorrow is a new day;
you shall begin it well and serenely.
-Ralph Waldo Emerson

Make a
Joyful Noise!

The crows are back!
After many years' absence…
the boisterous crew
with caws like rusty horns
confront morning mist.
Their bossy "Notice me!
Notice me!"
makes me thank
the grove of trees
for being home
to a noisy family
of tell-all crows.

Make a joyful noise unto the Lord.
-Psalm 98:4

Many things can bring us happiness–

good news, a special gift, a great vacation, an evening with friends. Yet more profound than happiness is joy, and joy comes from deep inside ourselves. Not dependent on what's happening around us, joy is a state of mind—an attitude that springs from a true appreciation of life and of being alive.

Joy allows us to embrace happiness as well as sorrow, and accept good times as well as not-so-good times with equal tranquility. It savors the wonders of the world and gives thanks for daily blessings for no other reason than because those things are here to be seen and experienced.

Peel away problems and fears, insecurities and obstacles, and there…at the core of your being…is joy.

*Enable me, dear God, to experience
long-lasting deep-down joy.
Amen*

Secret of Happiness

Julie Smith Thurston

My best friend makes me feel good about life—I guess that's why she's my best friend! Like a little songbird, Crystal knows how to pick up my spirits and brighten my whole day.

Once I asked her how she could be so happy all the time, and this is what she told me. "I wasn't always this way. In fact, I used to be kinda pouty. Then I met this girl in school who was always friendly and cheery, and I saw how she never lacked for friends. That's when I decided I wanted to be like her.

"From then on, I didn't go around wrapped up in my own thoughts. I practiced being happy, even if I wasn't. When I was around people, I thought about them instead of myself...and soon, I realized people liked to be around me. And then I felt happy for real.

"Sure, I've still got my down days, but then I think, 'What about this person, or that person? Maybe she's got a heavier load to carry than I have, and I want to be there for her to help her carry the weight. Even if it's just by saying something nice.' "

That's the day I learned Crystal's secret of happiness. "If she can do it," I said to myself, "so can I." And I did.

Joy is very infectious; therefore, be always full of joy.

-Mother Teresa

The sun does not shine for a few trees and flowers,
but for the wide world's joy.

-Henry Ward Beecher

If I keep a green bough in my heart,
the singing bird will come.

-Proverb

I will greatly rejoice in the Lord,
my soul shall be joyful in my God.

-Isaiah 61:10

Who is the happiest of men? He who values the merits
of others, and in their pleasure takes joy, even as
though it were his own.

-Johann Wolfgang von Goethe

Joy can be real only if people look upon their life as
a service, and have a definite object in life outside
themselves and their personal happiness.

-Leo Tolstoy

In Perfect Harmony

The birds have flown,
and the nest fell down
in an early-winter storm.
Tightly woven twigs
and downy feathers…
a perfect sphere
of family love.

For the LORD thy God hath blessed
thee in all the works of thy hand.
-Deuteronomy 2:7

A perfect nest...a perfect egg...a perfect
bird...and you pick up pen or charcoal...paint, thread,
or camera...break into song or dance. "Whoa!" you
say, "not me!" Because you tried once, and a teacher
smirked, a classmate snickered...and fear made your
spirit shrink like a summer-wilted rose.

If you try again, will it be perfect? No. Only God is
perfect, and only He creates perfect things. But He has
showered you with talents and gifts and the desire to
create...He has sprinkled inspiration all around you.
The only real "imperfection" is not to reach out...to
do....to let yourself try.

Dear God, grant me the courage it takes to
express the thoughts and stories of my heart.
Amen

A Little Bird Told Me

Genoa Sherman

It was the picture of embarrassment. What I had drawn for a face looked more like a pie plate, and features lay across its pane like misplaced apple seeds. While the rest of the class had grasped what our teacher taught us about perspective, I didn't get it. Needless to say, Art II was not on my class schedule the next term, or any term to follow.

Years later, the local library offered a beginner art class for adults, and on impulse, I signed up. "What's to lose?" I told myself, adding that perhaps adulthood had endowed me with sufficiently thick skin to ward off immobilizing shame. In truth, I really wanted to learn how to draw.

Start-day came, and I was among 14 would-be artists sitting in the designated room. I noticed that most of us were shifting nervously in our chairs, twiddling with our art supplies, and avoiding looking directly at anyone. For the first session, our instructor suggested we go outside and sketch. "Draw whatever you see," he told us. "Don't analyze it, judge it, or edit it—just relax and let yourself go."

So we traipsed into a small park next to the library, each of us choosing a bench, rock, stump, or patch of grass to sit on. I was determined to follow instructions and not even think about the finished product, but simply enjoy the process.

At that moment, a little brown wren sailed above me and landed on the branch of a bush not six feet away. Immediately, I began to sketch. I became so engaged with the wren, swept up in the thrill of catching an enchanted moment on paper, of mindfully noticing her beak, her breast, her wings, and her up-tilted tail, that I was startled when the instructor called us back together.

Now it was time for show and tell. Almost every drawing was prefaced with an apology. "This isn't very good, but..." "Mine is probably the worst in the class..." "I can't draw at all, so..." At that point, I realized that we were the brave ones, standing in front of the class, our drawing in hand. How many other women and men, I wondered, didn't sign up for the class because someone had told them—or they told themselves—that they "aren't very good" or "can't draw"? How many wanted to draw, but were afraid to try?

Without apology, I put on a smile as I held up the picture of my little wren. Tension dissipated and smiles flowed. Was my drawing good? Was it bad? That's up to the observer. As for me, I hung it on the door of my refrigerator. Whenever I think I can't do something, I look at the little bird who always tells me to try.

Use what talents you possess: the woods would be very silent if no birds sang there except those that sang best.

-Henry Van Dyke

Perfection consists in one thing alone,
which is doing the will of God.
-Vincent de Paul

We must have perseverance and above
all confidence in ourselves. We must believe
that we are gifted for something, and that this thing,
at whatever cost, must be attained.
-Marie Curie

It is reasonable to have perfection
in our eye that we may always advance toward it,
though we know it can never be reached.
-Samuel Johnson

A Touch of Beauty in a Wintery Scene

Dark winds howled
throughout the night,
and what the weather
forecaster declared
in dire, warning tones—
it snowed.
I woke to the expected
3-5 inches,
surveyed the silent whited yard,
punctuated by a whistled peep
and a dot of red—
life!—
perched high in the frame
of a skeletal tree.

A thing of beauty is a joy forever.
-John Keats

In many regions, the seasons bring marked changes not only to the temperature outside, but to the garden. Flowers sprout, grow, bloom, then fade… grass greens, flourishes, then lies dormant until the early spring rains. Birds arrive in trickles, then in flocks…they raise their families, then fly away as days shorten and winds chill.

Seasonal changes compel us to notice…notice what's different…what has gone, what has come. What is beautiful about one season disappears, only to bring about something else beautiful, unique to that time of year. After all, who would want to compare the beauty of a rose in summer with that of a cardinal in winter? They are both exquisite in their own time.

Beauty may change with all life's seasons…but beauty is there in each one.

Dear God, bring me to see and appreciate the beauty of each stage and circumstance of my life.

Amen

Girl Plans, God Laughs

Patricia Mitchell

"I miss the changing of the seasons," a transplanted classmate moaned, and I had no idea what she was talking about. Born and raised in Southern California, I knew only "hot" (most of the time) and "cold" (anything below 60). When the school principal declared "inclement weather," he meant it was raining and girls could wear slacks to school (and it didn't happen very often.)

Palm trees never lost their palms, and lawn-mowing was a year-round activity. An autumn backyard bonfire would have brought out the entire fire department in our edge-of-desert town east of Lost Angeles. If I needed to wear a coat to church on Christmas Eve, I was annoyed. When my classmate informed me that, where she came from, she often wore a coat on Easter Sunday, I was appalled. "Never," I told myself, "never will I ever live in the Midwest, seasons or no seasons!"

Over 30 years ago, the Midwest is precisely where life took me, and where I'm still living. It took only one year here for me to know what my former classmate was saying when she said, "I miss the changing of the seasons." How could anyone not?

Each season unfolds in its time, bringing its unique sights and sounds, flavors and fragrances. There's the miracle of tiny green buds peeking up from a patch of melting snow... the luxurious perfume of my neighbor's verbena floating on an early spring breeze...lush carpets of flowers spread across verdant hills...the meditative stillness of evergreens wrapped in snow. When one season closes, another opens...just like last year, but different, too, with untold events, ideas, and discoveries in front of me.

Before I left California, a coworker said this to me: "Home is where you have your home and family, your work and church." I have discovered all those things here...and the seasons, too.

As for the temperature on Easter Sunday...it's not exactly balmy. I remember my classmate as I put on my coat...and boots.

> *Though we travel the world to find the beautiful,*
> *we must carry it with us or we find it not.*
> *-Ralph Waldo Emerson*

An Appreciative Eye for Beauty

To act with common sense,
according to the moment,
is the best wisdom I know;
and the best philosophy
is to do one's duties,
take the world as it comes,
submit respectfully to one's lot,
and bless the goodness that has
given us so much happiness with it,
whatever it is.

-Horace Walpole

Not my will, but thine be done.
Luke 22:42

We know how we wanted things to turn out—but they didn't. There are two ways we can respond.

One way is to reject the outcome because it doesn't match our hopes and desires. We can turn away in disgust, having nothing to do with a situation so entirely different from what we feel might have happened... and should have happened.

Another way is to accept reality. Though we may disapprove, our acceptance gives us the perspective we need to manage new conditions, and even take responsible measures to effect a better solution. Acceptance may put us face-to-face with hard truths, but acceptance also gives us the power to find a better way. And sometimes acceptance opens our eyes to unexpected goodness, beauty, and blessings.

> *Dear God, enable me to accept Your will in all aspects of my life.*
> *Amen*

Designed by Mother Nature

T. R. Cunningham

Last spring, and several previous springs, I had every inten-
tion of taming my garden. The lilac bushes needed thinning,
and I wanted to pull up the roots of an invasive grass before
it got established again. I planned to put down another layer
of mulch to deter weeds, and then, throughout spring and
summer, pull out unwelcome thistles and other volunteer
vegetation.

A few out-of-town conferences and long workdays completely squelched my best intentions. By midsummer, the lilacs
were bushier than ever, and various tall grasses, broad-
leafed stalks, wildflowers, and weeds were thriving. "Too
late to do much about it," I sighed, realizing that another
season was quickly drawing to a close, and still my garden
nowhere near the tidy plot I had in mind.

Perhaps it was the angle of the sun that made everything
different the other day…but a walk across my garden was
like stepping into another world. Myriad shades of green
enchanted me, and everywhere I looked, I saw life—
sparrows flitting and fluttering in a web of swaying limbs
upraised in a glorious dance of praise…a spotted toad

nestled in the mulch and contemplating the world, barely
visible in the verdant shadows…butterflies hovering over
a cluster of coneflowers…a sunflower, nearly picked clean
by the neighborhood cardinals, nodding in the early
autumn breeze.

For the first time, I truly enjoyed my garden—its abundance,
its exuberance, its carefree existence bursting with the pleasure of life. Was it out-of-control? Most definitely—and that,
too, was part of its splendor.

There are joys which long to be ours.
God sends ten thousands truths, which come about us like
birds seeking inlet; but we are shut up to them, and so they
bring us nothing, but sit and sing awhile upon the roof,
and then fly away.
-Henry Ward Beecher

Make a virtue of necessity.
-Geoffrey Chaucer

To expect life to be tailored to our
specifications is to invite frustration.
-Saying

With a Little Help from Friends

Cupped in my hands
the little thing fluttered
as the cat watched warily,
perhaps angry
I had interrupted his play
but resigned to give way
to the tall woman who carried
his frightened prey
to higher ground.

Encourage one another and build each other up,
just as in fact you are doing.
-1 Thessalonians 5:11 NIV

Our friends help, support, and encourage us
more times than we can imagine. They listen as we
pour out our frustrations, and they understand in ways
others never will. Friends are the ones we depend on
to be there for us, to be on our side, and to care about
what we're going through.

In even a deeper way, God offers His friendship to
you. When you turn to Him in prayer, you will find
Him there to listen and understand...when your heart
reaches out to Him, He responds with His tender love
for you. Like a best friend ever, He is there for you...
always.

*Today, dear God, let Your presence and Your
friendship fill my heart with strength,
encouragement, and love.*

Amen

"My" Red Tail Hawk

Mary Shields

We had been out of town for a few days and upon returning home, we thought we saw some kind of bird in the hostas around the large oak tree next to our driveway. Upon closer inspection, we saw it was a fledgling red tail hawk. I took a picture of it, thinking it was a rare opportunity to get close and then it would fly away. After a few hours it was still there, but not wanting to mess with nature, we just left it alone.

The next morning we did not see the bird, but noticed quite a commotion across the street in our neighbor's yard. My husband went to see what was going on, and there was the fledgling hawk being dive bombed by every species of bird in the neighborhood! The next thing I knew, my husband was standing in our neighbor's yard with a squirt gun shooting at the dive-bombing birds! He looked like a wild man as he tried to buy the hawk time to get into the bushes to hide.

I decided to call a nature center to see how we could further help this bird. They said to watch where it went and they would be out the next day to pick it up. Easy for them to say! The next morning we looked for the bird, but it was nowhere in sight. I needed to get my mowing started, and while mowing I spotted the hawk fluttering around in another neighbor's yard.

Later in the day, a gal from the nature center came and picked up the bird. She promised she would keep in touch with us on its progress. She told us that it probably fell out of its nest before it had learned to fly. The parents either abandoned it or met some other fate.

After about eight weeks, the nature center called to say the hawk was doing great. It had been taught to fly and hunt and now was ready to be released. The next day, they brought the bird back to our yard and let it go free.

That was nearly three years ago. After being resettled, the red tail hawk soon found a mate, nested in the large oak tree by the driveway, and to this day regularly swoops over the neighborhood. I can't help but smile whenever I see "my" red tail hawk soaring high in the sky!

A Glad Heart

A comfy chair,
a sip of tea...
a robin outside my window
plucking blades of grass
for a tasty morsel
to bring home
to her waiting family...
yes, I have everything I need,
and my heart is glad.

He that is of a merry heart
hath a continual feast.
-Proverbs 15:15

"I'm glad for you!" We hear those words from others when we announce good news, like an engagement, well-deserved promotion, or long-desired dream-come-true. How often, however, do we express gladness in ordinary, everyday things?

In all likelihood, there's something you can see right now that makes you glad. Perhaps it's the face of a loved one...a familiar room...a cherished picture...a treasured souvenir...a flower blooming outside your window.

Let your heart be glad...let yourself say, "I'm glad today for me!"

Let my heart find gladness, dear God,
in the blessings You have so generously
given to me today.

                                        Amen

Our Kitchen with a View

Jeannie McDermott

My husband and I recently completed a minor remodeling of our kitchen. We know that anyone buying our house will probably rip everything out and start over, so we decided to keep our costs down and only replace the floor, counter tops, and stove. My husband was a little wistful about not adding a dishwasher since he does his share, and probably more, of dishwashing. However, it would have required some major redesign to fit one into our tiny kitchen.

Having never had a dishwasher, it isn't very hard for me to do without one. "Besides," I say to my husband, "think of all we would miss out on by not spending time in front of the kitchen window watching the events in our backyard."

A peanut feeder and thistle feeder hang within six inches of our kitchen window. Farther away is a suet feeder. All do a pretty steady business. When the temperatures dip way down in winter we usually see a row of sparrows fluffed up and snuggled together side-by-side on the sill of the south-facing window of our back room, enjoying what heat they can absorb from the thin winter sun.

The feeders next to the window occasionally provide a breathtaking show: a male red-bellied woodpecker at the peanut feeder. He is so large and so close that we can see all of his markings: the brilliant red-orange cap, the splotch of red-orange above his beak and even the faint blush on his breast that gives him his name.

The yard, too, provides entertainment as I scour the stubborn remains of oatmeal from its saucepan. Mourning doves toddle along, heads bobbing up and down like sewing machine needles. If we're lucky we might see a Carolina wren with his rich brown plumage and plucky manner, sifting through the ground cover below the suet feeder for a dropped morsel or two. The day wouldn't be complete without an acrobatic show by the squirrel and a quarreling band of starlings.

Very occasionally, we see the ruby crowned kinglet, a sighting that would be missed if it weren't for our sink full of dishes. This adorable speck of a bird reminds me of a figure skater as he effortlessly rises from the porch railing and alights on the feeder. If I were a bird, that is the bird I would want to be.

With spring comes the blooming of our white dogwood tree. Framed by the kitchen window it makes a magnificent picture. I open the window to let in the gentle spring breeze and smell the luscious scent of the lilac bush several feet to the right of the window.

As the spring progresses, a mama sparrow lands on the kitchen window feeder. Her newly fledged babies line up open-mouthed on the power line next to the feeder, pumping their wings and chirping for their fair share. This can be dangerous, as we observed one Sunday afternoon when my husband was washing and I was drying the lunch dishes. A kestrel swooped down below the feeder, snatched a mouse, and was gone in the blink of an eye! Baby sparrows, beware!

At dusk, I fill the kitchen sink with sudsy water. The sweet scent of honeysuckle wafts through the open window. When I turn off the water, I hear the last bird of the evening: the chi-ip, chi-ip, chi-ip of the nearby cardinal. I am glad we didn't get a dishwasher. As boring as scrubbing pots and drying silverware can be, I think I won't trade my time in front of the kitchen window for a shiny new dishwasher.

Pleasure is very seldom found where it is sought.
Our brightest blazes are commonly
kindled by unexpected sparks.
-Samuel Johnson

*A contented mind is the greatest blessing
a man can enjoy in this world.*
-Joseph Addison

If you want to be happy, be.
-Leo Tolstoy

*What a wonderful life I've had!
I only wish I'd realized it sooner.*
-Colette

To Seek...
and to Find

Keep the currents moving.
Don't let your life stagnate.

-John Burroughs

Ask, and it shall be given you;
seek, and ye shall find;
knock, and it shall be opened unto you.

-Matthew 7:7

Change is rarely easy. Even when welcome change comes into our lives, it brings new expectations, new goals, new challenges, and new routines to adopt. Change also tempts us to look back and imagine a past when things were perfect and we had fewer problems—a past we know never truly existed.

Whether wanted or unwanted, change comes, and it compels you to go forward. Change thrusts you into unfamiliar territory, and at the same time creates opportunities you may never have imagined would come your way. Let change be the catalyst that allows you to discover, explore, and grow.

Dear God, prepare my mind to seek and my heart to find the blessings You have put before me today.

Amen

The Empty Nest

Madison McRobert

I'm not sure your chick is ready to leave the nest, mama. As I watch the mama robin nudge her chick to try her little wings, I can't help but remember how I felt the day my youngest left our nest. Only two months ago, she was a high schooler doing her homework to the thump, thump, thump of "music"...changing her outfit again and again, and still fretting she wasn't wearing the right thing...concerned less about grades sometimes than whether or not the cute boy in English Lit liked her.

She thought she was ready to leave, of course. In fact, she couldn't wait. She shrieked with joy to read her college acceptance letter. The day we moved her things into her dorm room, I dawdled before leaving...but when there was nothing left to rearrange or pack away, I realized I could put if off no longer. I hugged my baby and said good-bye. The tears didn't start coming until I heard her softly close the door behind me.

I remember returning to the house, now strangely silent... no more footsteps in the kitchen at all hours, no one chattering on the phone all evening, no forgotten lights gleaming in the basement. For the first few nights, I was at a loss for what to do. Sure, I was proud of her for working hard to get into the college of her choice, and I looked forward to meeting the lovely, accomplished woman she would become...but I mourned those first few days. I mourned deeply.

"Hi mom what r u doing?" was a message she sent, and the one that stared at me like a mirror, a mirror reflecting the person I didn't want to be...the one who does nothing but sit and wish and dream and clasp old memories, as if holding on to them will make those times come back. No, that wouldn't be me. I picked up the phone and called a friend who volunteered at the community college.

Within the hour, I had a reply for her. I told her I'd be tutoring ESL classes three mornings a week. My training session was set for this evening...so bye, hon...love u!

Yes, mama robin, everything will be all right with your little one. See...whooo! Look at her take to the air! Now, how about you? What does the rest of your day look like?

> Change is the watchword of progression.
> When we tire of well-worn ways, we seek for new.
> This restless craving in the souls of men
> Spurs them to climb, and seek the mountain view.

from *The Year Outgrows the Spring*
Ella Wheeler Wilcox

God's Presence Yesterday, Today, and Forever

In the early morning hours
when darkness hovers
like an ominous cloud
an owl calls
from the rooftop,
breaking the spell
of night and promising
the break of day.

As a mother comforts her child,
so will I comfort you.
-Isaiah 66:13 NIV

Have you ever felt alone and afraid? Most of us have at some point in life. Alone in the house, we heard a window break downstairs...alone with our thoughts, anxiety magnified an issue to frightening pro-portions...alone in the night, it seemed the morning light would never come.

An awareness of God's presence comforts and soothes us in these times of intense loneliness. His is the light that leads us through dark times...times we were never meant to go through all by ourselves. Faith in Him...faith in His loving, protective presence...gives us the strength and courage we need every time...at all times.

When I am in darkness, dear God,
embrace me in Your protective arms.
                                    Amen

When the Sparrow Falls

Carole Ann Blackley

From my window I saw them huddled together on the ground, nearly blending with the mulch I had piled on the path. As quietly as I could, I stepped outside to get a better look. A little smaller than a finch, the pair of tiny feathered creatures didn't budge as I drew closer. I saw no sign of injury, yet these two seemed in no hurry to find higher ground.

While longing to help, yet wondering what to do, I noticed they had already attracted the attention of my two cats, who were peering intently out the window. Their interest brought to mind my neighbor's kitten, a frisky indoor-outdoor fellow whose keen nose certainly would lead him straight to this spot as soon as he sniffed the breeze. Towering over the little helpless creatures, I felt like a feeble giant.

Their plight brought to mind a comment I once heard from a nonbelieving friend. Referring to Jesus' words in Matthew where He says that not even a sparrow falls to the ground without our Father's knowledge, she quipped, "Yet the sparrow still falls to the ground." To her, God was a heavenly giant, looking down from heaven and well-meaning, perhaps, but powerless to protect His fallen creatures.

Yes, there are the many "fallen sparrows" in every life—pain and hardship, harm and danger. Yet faith tells us this: God allows these things to happen, and nothing—and no one—suffers without His knowledge. Even more, He is still in control, even when we can't imagine why these things happen. I guess that's the meaning of faith—being willing to let God be God. My helplessness is mine, not His...my understanding is but a fraction of a penny compared to the wealth of His wisdom.

I went back into the house, and returned to the little birds (still not moved an inch) with a plate of water and a handful of seeds. I put these next to them, then backed away, all the while keeping an eye out for anything that might threaten them. I settled with a book in a patio chair where I could keep watch.

After about an hour, I looked up from my book, and I saw that most of the seed was gone. So were the birds. No, my friend, I don't know why they fell—but I do believe that they soared high into the sky again.

> *The light of God surrounds me,*
> *The love of God enfolds me,*
> *The power of God protects me,*
> *The presence of God watches over me,*
> *Wherever I am, God is.*
>
> *-Prayer*

Before me, even as behind, God is, and all is well.

-John Greenleaf Whittier

The will of God will not take you
where the grace of God cannot keep you.

-Saying

I believe in the incomprehensibility of God.

-Honoré de Balzac

Trust in the Lord with all thine heart;
and lean not unto thine own understanding.

-Proverbs 3:5

A humble knowledge of oneself is a surer road to God
than a deep searching of the sciences.

-Thomas à Kempis

*Be like the bird that, pausing on her flight awhile on
boughs too slight, feels them give way beneath her,
and yet sings, knowing that she hath wings.*

-Victor Hugo

The Lord delights in those who fear him,
who put their hope in his unfailing love.

-Psalm 147:11 NIV

A Work in Progress

Into the pine tree you dart
with a twig...a leaf...
a tuft of cottonwood tree.
Out you come,
little bird, perched again
on a topmost branch,
looking this way and that
for yet another treasure,
another gem
for this glorious
work in progress.

I can do all things through Christ which
strengtheneth me.
-Philippians 4:13

Seemingly effortlessly, a chef whips up a gourmet meal...a gymnast balances on a beam... an athlete finishes the race...a friend takes a handful of wildflowers and turns them into an elegant centerpiece. Have you ever watched while someone accomplished with ease a task you find difficult, if not impossible?

When we put to use the talents God has given to each of us, we acquire skill. Regular and dedicated practice gives us confidence, and with confidence comes increasing skill, and with increasing skill comes the ability to reach even higher levels of achievement.

It's not always difficult...once you've had a chance to practice.

*Dear God, help me make the most of the
skills You have given to me.*

Amen

Step by Step

Jean Hooper

Today I watched a sparrow construct her nest twig by twig. What dedication the little creature showed! Even when the twig was longer than she was, she held it firmly in her beak and disappeared into the evergreen bush. In a few seconds, she would fly out, empty-beaked, only to come back with another twig. Again and again, the busy little sparrow returned with something to add to her project.

The sparrow's willingness to build little by little, to go step by step, reminded me of something I have learned. Years ago, I would embark on a big project with enthusiasm, only to look up a short time later and realize I'd made hardly any progress. Then I would throw my hands up in defeat! Or I would look at someone else who was more advanced, and my heart would sink. "She does this so well," I'd pout, "but I can't!"

I tried to convince myself "I can't" was a fact, but I knew it was only an excuse. Of course I could if I'd try again...and again...and again. If I celebrated my small steps toward my goal rather than berating myself for not being at my goal.

If I'd put in the practice necessary to reach a higher level of accomplishment...if I understood that "little by little" can grow into something very big, indeed.

So now I keep at it, even if the going is slow. And who knows? I might inspire someone who for the first time is trying the stretching exercise I can do easily because I've been in the class for six months. Or the woman who buys the cookies I bake for the church fundraiser might decide to try her hand at baking again, despite last month's burnt cake.

I've often been inspired by someone not as all–knowing as the experts and professionals. The friend who took it upon herself to learn all she could about her computer and is now comfortable with technology shows me that I, too, can become the same way if I put in the time and effort.

These days, I let those who are ahead of me inspire rather than discourage me. I don't need to dash to where they are, or give up if I don't make it in record time. I've found deep satisfaction in moving forward step by step, giving it my best effort and building my ever-growing "nest" of skills as I go.

That which we persist in doing becomes easier—
not that the nature of the task has changed,
but our ability to do it has increased.
-Ralph Waldo Emerson

Let a man's talents or virtues be what they may, he
will only feel satisfaction as he is satisfied in himself.
-William Hazlitt

I'll walk where my own nature would be leading;
it vexes me to choose another guide.
-Emily Brontë

Wherever we are, it is but a stage on the
way to somewhere else, and whatever we do,
however well we do it, it is only a preparation to do
something else that shall be different.
-Robert Louis Stevenson

Leave results to God.
-Elizabeth Barrett Browning

Let perseverance finish its work so that you may be
mature and complete, not lacking anything.
-James 1:4 NIV

What exactly is success? For me it is to be
found not in applause, but in the satisfaction of feeling
that one is realizing one's ideal.
-Anna Pavlova

Nature never rhymes her children,
nor makes two men alike.
-Ralph Waldo Emerson

Better to do a little well than a great deal badly.
-Socrates

Going Home

As afternoon sunbeams
slant shadows across the field,
the flock gathers
and, with much ado,
takes to the sky
in multitudes.
A straggler follows,
a lone soul,
winging his way home
at last.

...I pray that you, being rooted and established
in love, may have power... to grasp how wide
and long and high and deep is the love of Christ.
-Ephesians 3:17-18 NIV

What does the word "home" mean

to you? Perhaps "home" means the town you grew up in or a house you moved away from many years ago. Or maybe you regard the place where you are right now as home, whether your time there has been days, years, or decades.

God calls your heart His home. He dwells in you no matter where you're living or where you are on your life's journey. It's His love for you that moves Him to live in you, and that's why His presence is never far. In fact, it's as close as your own heart.

Dear God, thank You for being with me
yesterday, today, and forever.
Amen

The Call of Home

The bride and groom, followed by the wedding party and their guests, gathered outside the church for the finale of their joyous ceremony. With a kiss and a wish known only to them, they released two white doves into the air. We ooohed! and aaaahed! as the pair fluttered high into the sky, followed by a flock of identical doves. Watching the birds soar into the clear afternoon sky made our hearts soar, too. What an exhilarating sight!

How apt a symbol for the couple's love that we pray will lift them high above snares and pitfalls! How the doves beautifully embody love's power to release kindness and joy, comfort and caring. And what a lovely way to remind us that married love never needs to "fly" alone—family and friends are there to help, support, and encourage through all the many seasons of love.

We watched in wonder as the doves circled and swirled, then, as if by a signal, each one turned and winged in the same direction, and then disappeared from sight behind a grove of trees. In a few more minutes, they would be gathered on a rooftop not far from the church at the place they come back to every time...the place called home.

The bird let loose in Eastern skies,
When hastening fondly home,
Ne'er stoops to earth her wing, nor flies
Where idle warblers roam;
But high she shoots through air and light,
Above all low delay,
Where nothing earthly bounds her flight,
Nor shadow dims her way.

So grant me, God, from every care
And stain of passion free,
Aloft, through Virtue's purer air,
To hold my course to Thee!
No sin to cloud, no lure to stay
My soul, as home she springs;
Thy sunshine on her joyful way,
Thy freedom in her wings!

-Thomas Moore

A Humble Heart

It is vain to gather
virtues without humility;
for the spirit of God
delighteth to dwell in the
hearts of the humble.

-Erasmus

The meek shall inherit the earth;
and shall delight themselves in the
abundance of peace.
-Psalm 37:11

In a world where it seems everyone craves the spotlight, a humble person really stands out! Yet to stand out—to call attention to herself—is the last thing humility seeks.

Rather than brag about her accomplishments, humility highlights the achievements of others; instead of constantly talking about herself, humility takes pleasure in listening. Humility accepts rightful praise with the same measure of grace that she receives constructive criticism, for to do anything else would marginalize the truth.

Yet the last thing humility talks about is humility... because to boast about humility just isn't humble, is it?

Empower me, dear God, to walk with
true humility today.

Amen

One in the Bush

Madison McRobert

After a few weeks of neglect, my garden turns into nothing short of a jungle! The plots I weeded and mulched at the beginning of spring cry for attention by the start of summer, and the top of the hedge I trimmed evenly straight across bristles with untamed growth. The little "pop-up trees" sprouting in my vegetable patch must go! An army of acorn-bearing squirrels must have wanted to plant a forest in my cucumbers.

A bright, sunny afternoon with a mild breeze brought me out, and I set about the tasks ahead of me. The neighborhood was quiet and peaceful—no cars, radios, barking dogs—and I breathed deeply the fresh, fragrant air, and I let the sounds of God's creation embrace me. The soft whispers of the fountain grasses as I pulled ground creepers from around the patio…the low murmur of the ancient oak as I gathered fallen limbs and twigs…the gentle rustle of the lilacs as I cleared away bloodroot and thistles…what singular luxury to know such peace!

It was then that a gentle chirp-chirp reached my ears. It was coming from the fully leaved river birch I planted last year. Chirp-chirp! Again, the sweet notes floated on the breeze brushing my spirit with a whisper of delicate beauty. Oh, I recognized the sound...it was the cardinal who regularly visits my feeder in search of sunflower seeds. Perhaps he was calling to his mate some ways away, as I've heard him do so often. Or perhaps he was chiding me for not replenishing the feeder with his favorite morsels this morning. Though the abundant leaves of the birch tree hid his bright red feathers, there was no mistaking his song.

The bird's willingness to sing without being seen...to share his song without calling for recognition...to give without asking for applause reminded me of those special people in my life who give so much, yet never interfere or push themselves forward. They're the ones who help and encourage me, serve and support me, and if I try to thank them, they'll say, "Oh, don't worry about it! It was no trouble at all!" And they truly mean it.

> *Conceit spoils the finest genius. There is not much danger that real talent or goodness will be overlooked long; even if it is, the consciousness of possessing and using it well should satisfy one.*
> *-Louisa May Alcott*

It is always the secure who are humble.
-G. K. Chesterton

*Blessed are those who can give without remembering
and take without forgetting.*
-Elizabeth Asquith Bibesco

Humility, like darkness, reveals the heavenly lights.
-Henry David Thoreau

*Be clothed with humility: for God resisteth the proud,
and giveth grace to the humble.*
-1 Peter 5:5

The higher we are placed,
the more humbly should we walk.
-Francois La Rochefoucauld

*True humility makes no pretense of being humble,
and scarcely ever utters words of humility.*
-Francis de Sales

These are a few of the ways we can practice humility:

Speak as little as possible of oneself.

Mind one's own business.

Avoid curiosity.

Do not want to manage other people's affairs.

Accept contradiction and correction cheerfully.

Pass over the mistakes of others.

Accept blame when innocent.

Yield to the will of others.

Accept insults and injuries.

Accept being slighted, forgotten and disliked.

Be kind and gentle even under provocation.

Do not seek to be specially loved and admired.

Never stand on one's dignity.

Yield in discussion even though one is right.

Choose always the hardest.

-Mother Teresa

Look to the Skies

I've dreamt in my life
dreams that have stayed
with me ever after,
and changed my ideas;
they've gone through
and through me,
like wine through water,
and altered the colour
of my mind.

-Emily Brontë

Great are the works of the Lord;
they are pondered by all who
delight in them.
-Psalm 111:2 NIV

A dazzling sunset over water...the life-saving
act of a hero...a tender blossom hidden among the
thorns...a baby's first smile...all these things stir us
to appreciate the splendor of our God-created world.
They inspire us to live more, feel more, smile more,
and love more.

God opens the eyes of our spirit through the words of
the Bible, inviting us to see for ourselves the beauty
of His love and to discover the power of His care
and compassion. His magnificent promises and His
comforting assurances release us from the fetters that
would keep us down. God empowers and inspires us
to live—to soar—in freedom!

Inspire me, dear God, to live more fully
and to see the beauty of every day.
Amen

The Eagle's Flight

Nadine Walker Williamson

"Hawk!" my four-year-old shouted while pointing to the sky, tracing with his finger the soaring creature. We came to a standstill, our feet planted in the cool damp sand of the lakeside beach.

"Oh, Davey," I exclaimed when I followed his gaze and spotted the bird's distinctive white head, massive wingspan, and long white tail features. "That's an eagle!" Both of us watched in awe as the magnificent bird took long circular swoops over the lake, his great wings carrying him from one side of the lake to the other with only a few graceful strokes.

"He's a big bird!" Davey announced solemnly.

"He sure is, honey," I said. "Do you see how strong he is? And how big and wide his wings are?"

Davey nodded, still looking as the eagle rose higher and higher into the sky. "God is big and strong like the eagle... even bigger and stronger," I told him. "He watches over us and sees where we are. And see how the eagle's shadow is on the lake?" Davey's eyes examined the water as the eagle's shadow silently swept from shore to shore. "We're like the eagle's shadow when we do what God does. When we help people, when we're kind and thoughtful, when we love each other, we're following God and doing what He does."

"Like the eagle's shadow!" Davey announced, looking up at me with a grin that never fails to melt my heart.

"Yes, like the eagle's shadow," I said. We looked up as the eagle took another circle around the lake, then disappeared from sight behind a grove of trees on the opposite shore. We continued our walk, feeling happy. We could sense that we were in the shadow of God's love.

When thou seest an eagle,
thou seest a portion of genius; lift up thy head!
-William Blake

If you wish to advance into the infinite,
explore the finite in all directions.
-Johann Wolfgang von Goethe

Vision is the art of seeing things invisible.
-Jonathan Swift

A Song of Heartfelt Gratitude

For lily pads and little frogs
and fireflies that glow...
for daisies in the summertime
and pine cones iced with snow...
for sparrows on the rooftop
and eagles on the wing...
for fragrant flowers
and peaceful hours...
thank You, God,
for everything.

If the only prayer you ever say in your entire
life is "Thank you," that would suffice.
-Meister Eckhart

"An attitude of gratitude" is more than a catchy way of reminding us to count our blessings. It goes deeper than that by inviting us to change the way we look at things. Rather than dwelling on what we lack, we're asked to focus on what we have. When we do, we discover how rich we are in so many ways—in physical possessions and spiritual gifts, in material blessings and in natural talents.

Not only does "an attitude of gratitude" bring contentment, it opens us to receive and enjoy even more of God's good gifts! It's no wonder that people who live with a heart rich in gratitude are rich in so many other ways, too.

Dear God, thank You for all the blessings You have showered on me this day.

Amen

The Mixed Bag

T. R. Cunningham

The bag of mixed seed seemed like a good buy. "Attracts a wide variety of wild birds," the label promised, and I could see the bag held plenty of sunflower seeds along with cracked corn, finch seed, and milo. Rather than set up several different feeders with various seeds, I would keep one large feeder filled with something for everybody!

Yes, there was something for everybody, but I quickly realized that gratitude is not part of a bird's vocabulary. The blue jay took immediate command of the feeder, scattering a dozen sparrows and finches. He hopped from one side of the perch to the other, digging through the tray for the sunflower seeds and with his beak, flinging the other seeds to the ground.

After the jay had his fill, he left without any further ado, freeing the feeder for his smaller, shier cousins. Back they came, and they, too, searched for their particular favorite by clearing away what they didn't want. By the end of the afternoon, more seed lay on the ground than in the feeder!

We're like those ungrateful birds when we grab the blessings we desire, but throw aside blessings we think we don't want or don't need.

Genuine gratitude for all God has given us enables us to accept with equal thanksgiving the good as well as the bad, the joyful as well as the painful experiences of life—the "mix" everyone's days and years never fail to bring. A grateful heart is in no danger of carelessly flinging aside a blessing, or of dismissing a blessing God wants to put into our lives. When we receive all with gratitude, we quickly learn that unfamiliar seeds are often delightful treats, and openness to new ideas brings many happy surprises.

"Thank you" are two small words, but in them lie the seeds of a happy, abundant life.

> *My debt to you, Beloved,*
> *Is one I cannot pay*
> *In any coin of any realm*
> *On any reckoning day.*
> -*Jesse Belle Rittenhouse*

I will praise the name of God with a song,
and will magnify him with thanksgiving.
-Psalm 69:30

*The person who has stopped being
thankful has fallen asleep in life.*
-Robert Louis Stevenson

When I first open my eyes upon the morning meadows
and look out upon the beautiful world,
I thank God I am alive.
-Ralph Waldo Emerson

*Our real blessings often appear to us
in the shape of pains, losses and disappointments.*
-Joseph Addison

Ingratitude is a kind of weakness;
the clever are never ungrateful.
-French proverb

Reflect upon your present blessings,
of which every man has many;
not on your past misfortunes,
of which all men have some.
-Charles Dickens

Man's chief work is to praise God.
-Augustine

Be glad of life because it gives you the chance to love
and to work and to play and to look up at the stars.
-Henry Van Dyke

Sunshine is delicious, rain is refreshing, wind braces us
up, snow is exhilarating; there is really no such thing
as bad weather, only different kinds of good weather.
-John Ruskin

All which we behold is full of blessings.
-William Wordsworth

We can do no great things—
only small things with great love.

-Mother Teresa